'There She Blows'

Sealing & Whaling Days in New Zealand

Sarah Ell

THE BUSH PRESS OF NEW ZEALAND

First published in 1995 by
THE BUSH PRESS

Designed by Gordon Ell, and produced by The Bush Press in Auckland.
Printed in Hong Kong through Bookprint Consultants Ltd, Wellington, N.Z.

Published by Bush Press Communications Ltd, P.O.Box 33-029, Takapuna, Auckland 9, N.Z.

ISBN 0-908608-24-1

ACKNOWLEDGEMENTS
The author and publishers thank the Alexander Turnbull Library of the National Library of New Zealand and the Hocken Library of the University of Otago, for historic illustrations as credited. Thanks also to Mark Solomon and Whale Watch Kaikoura Ltd, for the colour pictures of whales on page 48 and on the cover. Colour pictures of seals and of former whaling stations are by Gordon Ell, A.R.P.S.
The maps and original drawings are by Jo Kensington.
Thanks particularly to Mike Donoghue of the Department of Conservation for his generous help and advice.

Contents

Steel engraving from Henry T. Cheever's The Whaleman's Adventures in the Southern Ocean *(1850).*
ALEXANDER TURNBULL LIBRARY

The 'South Seas Fishery'

The first European visitors to New Zealand were drawn by its natural riches. Soon after Lieutenant James Cook's rediscovery of the islands, ships began to visit New Zealand shores in search of timber, flax, seals, and whales.

Before the arrival of Europeans, the waters about New Zealand were home to countless thousands of great whales and seals. Cook recorded the presence of both in his journals.

When Cook visited Dusky Sound in Fiordland, aboard the *Resolution* in 1773, he noted that fur seals were plentiful about the coast. Seals were killed so the crew could have fresh meat. Seal oil was used for lamp fuel and their hides to mend the ship's rigging.

Less than 20 years later, the first sealing expedition visited New Zealand. A party of 12 men were put ashore at Dusky Sound in 1792, and spent a year there, collecting 4500 seal skins for the Chinese market. Yet little more than 30 years later, the sealing trade was all but finished, the 'robber industry' killing itself by practically exterminating the seals.

As sealing faded away, it was replaced by another extractive industry, whaling. The first shore whaling stations were established in southern New Zealand in the late 1820s, while British, Australian, American and French whaleships worked in northern waters from the same period. New Zealand also became a reprovisioning point for whaleships working the larger South Seas whale fishery, stretching north to Fiji and Tonga.

The slaughter of right and sperm whales in New Zealand waters was fast and furious — and quickly over. By the time New Zealand became a British colony, in 1840, most of the right whales which frequented its coastline were dead, and the whalers had moved on.

Left: Fur seal basks on a breakwater near Otago Heads.

PHOTOGRAPHS: GORDON ELL

Left: Fur seals on Breaksea Island, Fiordland. Lieutenant James Cook noted the presence of seals in the area in 1773. Within 20 years sealing gangs from Sydney began work on the New Zealand coast. After nearly 200 years, fur seal populations are still recovering from the harvest.

FISH OR MAMMAL?

People once thought whales were fish. They did not know, as we do today, that whales and seals are in fact mammals. Although they live in the sea, they breathe air, are warm-blooded and give birth to live young, just like mammals which live on the land.

The Maori and Seals and Whales

Seals and whales were once much more plentiful about the New Zealand coast. In warmer times, seals bred around the coast of the North Island as well as the South and Stewart Islands. Their bones and teeth are often found in the remains of ancient rubbish tips and campfire sites. Maori who lived near seal colonies on the coast killed fur seals for their meat and blubber, for food, and for their skins, which could be made into warm clothing.

The whale was considered a 'chiefly fish' by the Maori, a symbol of bounty. A stranded whale produced a wealth of food and highly-prized whale bone, used to make implements and ornaments. Sometimes small whales were driven to strand in the shallows by Maori, but more often an accidental stranding was seen as a lucky blessing.

The migration legends of many tribes feature whales, as a sign for the tribe to settle in a certain place, or acting either as a guide or, in the case of Paikea, a mode of transport from Hawaiki. Some lucky individuals were said to have a whale as a 'guardian spirit' watching over them at sea. The stylised shapes of whales were often carved on the barge boards of special storage houses, symbolising the bounty within.

The Maori called the right whale *kewa* and the sperm whale *paraoa*. The name Whangaparaoa, used for bays both just north of Auckland and inside Cape Runaway at East Cape, means 'bay of the sperm whales'.

Pendants carved from the teeth of sperm whales, *rei puta*, were highly prized by the Maori. Whale bone was also carved into clubs, cloak pins and combs.

Rei puta, a form of Maori neck pendant which is traditionally carved from a whale's tooth.

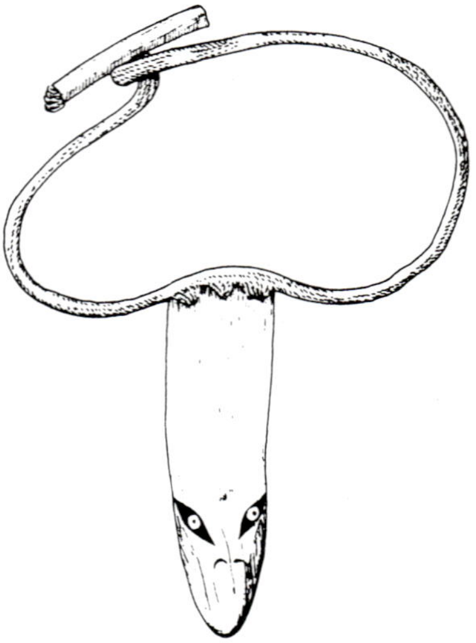

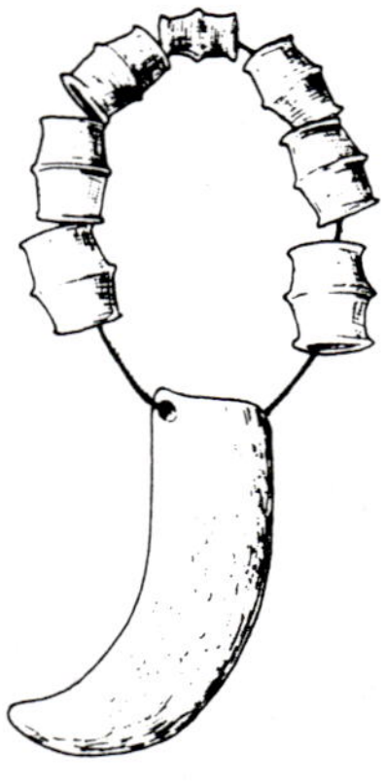

Paikea, the whale rider. The ancestral figure atop this meeting house at Whangara, East Cape, recalls the journey of Paikea to Aotearoa on the back of a whale.

Seal types

Sea lion

The main type of seal hunted on the New Zealand coast by Europeans was the fur seal *Arctocephalus forsteri*. It was once widely spread around the South Island coastline, but today its main breeding grounds are on the west coast of the South Island, Stewart Island, the Chatham Islands and the sub-Antarctic islands further south, although there are non-breeding winter colonies further north. It is also found in Australia, as far west as Perth.

The fur seal is carnivorous, feeding on squid and fish. Its coat of fur consists of an outer layer of coarse guard hairs which traps an insulating layer of air and water within a soft and dense underfur — an efficient method of heat retention while swimming. This layer of fur enables the fur seal to live in cold climates and swim in cold seas — but it also made them attractive to the sealers, who killed them for their skins.

Fur seals come ashore to specific breeding colonies or rookeries on rocky coastlines in southern New Zealand in summer. The males wander further north to 'hauling-out' grounds in winter.

By contrast, sea lions (or hair seals) choose sandy beaches on which to come ashore to breed. The sea lion hunted in New Zealand was the Hooker's sea lion *Phocarctos hookeri*, now one of the world's rarest seal species. It is found rarely on the mainland South Island, and breeds only on the sub-Antarctic islands, mainly Auckland Island.

The elephant seal *Mirounga leonina* was also hunted by European sealers. With adult males weighing more than 3000kg, it was a formidable prey. It was sought mainly for its oil, extracted by boiling the thick layer of blubber. The sea elephant was mainly slaughtered on Macquarie Island, an isolated island in the sub-Antarctic Southern Ocean, now part of Australia.

Elephant seal

DRAWINGS:JO KENSINGTON

The First European Sealers

Sealers were the first Europeans to settle in New Zealand, even if only for a few months or years. The party of sealers put ashore in Dusky Sound in 1792 created the first recorded European settlement here, building huts and starting work on a small ship to take them back to Sydney.

The sealing trade in New Zealand remained somewhat slow over the next decade however, as the New South Wales-based gangs exploited the seal grounds in Bass Strait, between mainland Australia and Tasmania. By the early years of the nineteenth century, however, the seal ships were back, in search of new grounds around the Southland and Fiordland coasts of the South Island and the islands further south: Auckland, Campbell, Macquarie, the Antipodes. Joining the slaughter were efficient American crews, but they were not as prevalent here as in Bass Strait.

Few official records exist to show the places the sealers visited, for the gangs and their employers were very secretive to stop rivals encroaching on their grounds. Underhand means were sometimes employed to 'poach' good sealing grounds.

Sealing gangs illustrated in Foreign field sports, fisheries, sporting anecdotes *(1814).*
ALEXANDER TURNBULL LIBRARY

Killing the Seals

The seals were clubbed as they lay ashore in their colonies. Sealers quietly approached their quarry from downwind to avoid detection, but once they were amongst the animals it was 'commonly the custom to set up a yell to confuse them...' wrote John Boultbee, a sealer who visited the South Island in the 1820s. 'Then begins the slaughter, the men hitting right and left as fast as they can with their clubs, until there is not a seal left.' The seals were clubbed on the head, on a 'soft spot' between the eyes.

The job was not nearly as dangerous as whaling. Although the men were attacking large, adult seals the animals were somewhat cumbersome on land. The sealing gangs had to keep a watch on the breaking surf, however.

Once the seals were dead, the men worked quickly to skin them and prepare the hides. For the European and American markets some blubber was left on before the skins were salted, while the Chinese demanded their seal skins be scraped completely clean. The hides were pegged out to dry with long wooden pegs, cut from nearby vegetation.

Later, when the seal population was depleted and the animals more wary of humans, they were sometimes shot from a short distance instead of clubbed. Boultbee also mentions 'spearing' an old seal deep in a cave with a knife bound to the end of a stick.

Lances, such as those used in whaling, were also sometimes used. The lance was either poked or thrown to pierce the seal under the left front flipper and thus stab it in the heart.

The fur seal was the main species taken by sealers on the New Zealand coast.
DRAWING: JO KENSINGTON

The Sealing Life

The men who chose the sealing life were a mixed bunch: mostly 'currency lads', as the first Australian-born Europeans were called, but also ex-convicts, British, North and South Americans, Australian aborigines and Portuguese.

The sealers worked for 'lays' or shares of the catch, and took pride in their 'self-employment'. The men had to be tough, resourceful and disciplined to gather and preserve skins and keep themselves fed and housed in extreme conditions.

Some sealers lived in rough huts or tents, others under over-turned boats. A cave could make a good shelter. Some gangs tried to grow vegetables, but the sites which the seals frequented seldom made good gardens. Instead, the sealers' diet consisted of salt rations, seal meat, fish and fern root, and sometimes the eggs of seabirds. Native birds such as the weka or ducks were also eaten. As a last resort many of the islands were well populated with rats.

Sometimes the sealing gangs were befriended by local Maori; at other times they were attacked by the original occupants of the land. Three deserters from a gang in Foveaux Strait were killed and eaten, 'and thus sadly atoned for their desertion'. As a boy, James Caddell survived the massacre of the rest of his party when he fell under *tapu* by touching the cloak of the attacking chief. John Boultbee's *Journal of a Rambler* gives a vivid account of an attack by night by a Maori raiding party, in which two Europeans were killed.

It is hard to imagine why men would have chosen such a life. Still, it was less dangerous than whaling, an adventurous alternative to farming, and less disciplined than shipboard life. The main motivation for many sealers may well have been money, however; a contemporary observer wrote: 'How powerful must be the love of gain, when it can induce men to support the fatigues and privations which fall to the lot of the seal fishers.'

Sealing gangs were sometimes castaway on remote reefs or islands. 'He raised his arms towards Heaven and uttered a cry' — a castaway rescued, from Les Naufrages des Iles Auckland, *by F. E. Raynal.*
ALEXANDER TURNBULL LIBRARY

John Boultbee's Journal of a Rambler *is one of the few accounts of the industry written by an educated sealer. He spent almost two years working around the coasts of Fiordland and Southland from 1826.*

Castaways

It was not uncommon for sealing ships to set down a gang on an isolated island or beach and return to Sydney for reprovisioning. The ship might not return for months or, if lost at sea, not at all.

In 1813 a gang of sealers was rescued from the rocky outcrop of Solander Island, in Foveaux Strait. Some of the men had been there for more than four years. A report in the Sydney *Gazette* said the men were 'cloathed in seal skins, of which their bedding was also composed, and their food had been entirely made up from the flesh of the seal, a few fish occasionally caught, and a few sea birds that now and then frequent the island... They had long endured calamity, but had until within the last few months of their relief, entertained some hope of succour, which from a length of disappointment had gradually immerged into a state of entire hopelessness.'

Captain John Grono rescued a group from Jackson Bay, Westland, who had been marooned for three years after their ship, the *Active*, went missing. The castaways had killed 11,000 seals and preserved 8,700 skins, and had begun carving boards from tree trunks to build a ship, when rescued in 1813. Grono took the survivors to his home, and three of them married three of his daughters.

CAPTAIN GRONO

Captain John Grono was a Sydney shipbuilder who helped shape the early years of sealing in New Zealand. Grono was born in Newport, Wales in 1763 and learned the maritime trades in the Royal Navy.

He made his first sealing voyage to southern New Zealand in 1808, returning six months later with a cargo of 10,000 skins. Grono set up a series of sealing huts and camps, with slipways to enable boats to be pulled from the West Coast surf to safety. In the 1810s, three voyages produced 35,000 skins.

In the course of his sealing expeditions, Grono explored much of the west coast of the South Island. His voyages live on in names such as Milford and Caswell Sounds, named after harbours in his homeland.

Grono quickly became a respected expert on the New Zealand sealing grounds, and men who served with him were sought-after as pilots for other sealing vessels.

The New Zealand sealing grounds extended down the west coast of the South Island to the islands and reefs about Stewart Island. Gangs also worked the sub-Antarctic Islands to the south and southwest of New Zealand.
MAP: JO KENSINGTON

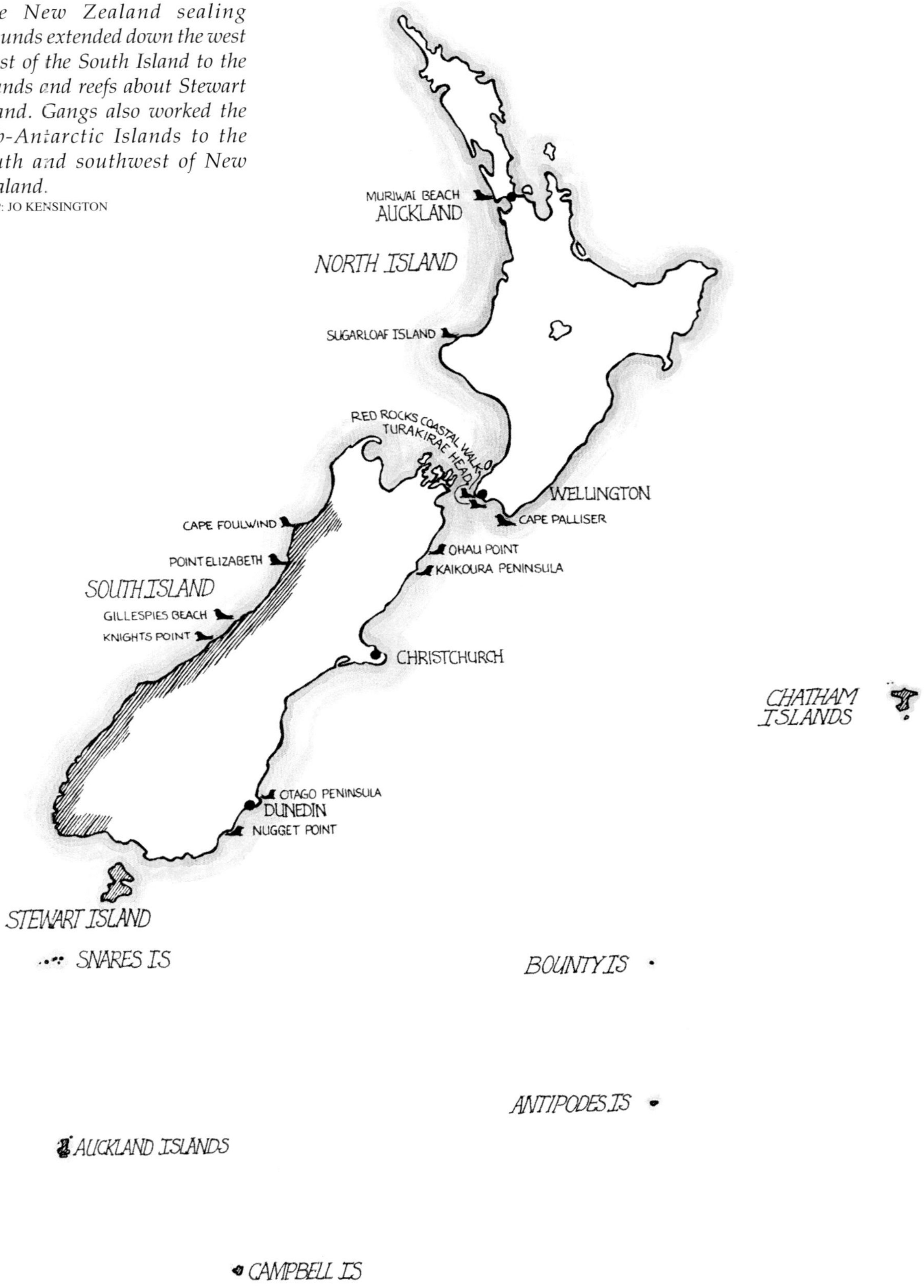

Sealing in Decline

It was inevitable that such a destructive industry should eventually kill itself. By the 1820s the huge populations of fur seals on the New Zealand coast were almost all gone, and it became uneconomic to mount sealing expeditions.

Sealing lasted on the islands south of New Zealand into the early 1820s. Many sealers then turned to whaling, using their knowledge of New Zealand and its marine environment to good advantage. Some small-scale sealing, sometimes in the off-season at shore whaling stations, persisted into the 1840s.

Some voyages in the first decade of the nineteenth century had returned with huge numbers of skins, such as the *Favourite* in 1806 which gathered 60,000 skins. However, the total number of seal skins imported into Sydney in 1830 was just 9700. By 1840 this number had dropped to just 470.

Isolated sealing continued into this century. The fur seal was given full protection in 1894, but this was lifted several times to allow limited seasons under licence. The last commercial season was as late as 1946. Since September 30 that year, no sealing has been allowed in New Zealand waters.

Seals Today

The seal population has slowly increased since the slaughter of the eighteenth century. Today there are an estimated 50,000-100,000 fur seals in New Zealand waters and colonies in Bass Strait and South Australia.

The Hooker's sea lion is still considered a 'vulnerable' species, with a population estimated at between 10,000-14,000.

Elephant seals, which occasionally come ashore in New Zealand, are also rare, and scientists believe their population is still declining in some parts of their range.

All species of seal, as well as all other marine mammals, are protected under the Marine Mammals Protection Act. It is an offence to disturb or harass seals — as well as being potentially dangerous.

Today there are several places around the New Zealand coast where fur seals can be seen (marked by seal symbol on the map). There are major colonies, some with viewing facilities, around the Wellington and Wairarapa coasts, at Kaikoura, in Otago and on the west coast of the South Island. Wandering young males are reported more widely about the coast, especially in haul-out areas in winter.

The Great Whales

The great whales of the sea, and their smaller relatives the dolphins and porpoises, are collectively called cetaceans. This group of marine mammals is divided into two Orders: Mysteceti, the baleen whales, and Odontoceti, the toothed whales. The two main types of whale hunted in New Zealand waters in the nineteenth century were the right whale and the sperm whale. In the twentieth century, with the development of motor vessels and the explosive harpoon gun, the whalers turned to the faster-swimming humpback whale.

The southern right whale *Eubalaena australis* is one of the baleen whales, which eat plankton filtered from ocean water through large horny plates suspended from the upper jaw. The word baleen comes from the Greek word for 'moustached', referring to the horny 'hairs' which fringe the baleen rods and filter the whales' food. Baleen whales have two blow holes on top of the head.

Right whale

The southern right whale grows up to 18m long and can weigh up to 70 tonnes. Almost half its body weight is fat and blubber. The right whale is purplish-black in colour and its head is often dotted with white growths of whale lice, barnacles and parasitic worms. It was the 'right' whale to hunt because it was relatively slow-moving, floated well when dead, and produced large quantities of valuable oil and baleen.

The right whale was once common around the shores of New Zealand and throughout the southern hemisphere, but it was hunted almost to extinction last century. Now these whales are found only in a few areas, such as off Argentina, South Africa, South Australia and the sub-Antarctic islands south of New Zealand.

DRAWINGS: JO KENSINGTON

Sperm whale

The sperm whale or cachalot *Physeter macrocephalus* is the largest of the toothed whales. Adult males grow up to 20m long and may weigh up to 58 tonnes, much larger and heavier than their mates. The sperm whale's head makes up one-third of its body size, and within it is the reserve of spermaceti oil from which the whale gets its name. The sperm whale is black or dark brown, and has a single blow-hole at the front of its enormous head. When it spouts, the stream of condensation is emitted at a 45 degree angle, making the species easy to identify.

Huge teeth line its lower jaw, with which it can bite but not chew. The sperm whale hunts deep in the ocean for fish, squid, and octopus; many whales bear sucker-marks as testimony of battles with their prey.

Humpback whale

Breeding in the tropical south Pacific and feeding each summer in the Antarctic, the humpback whale *Megaptera novaeangliae* was killed by whalers on its migration through New Zealand waters. The whalers soon discovered it was better to kill the humpbacks on their way north, after a feeding season. Also a baleen whale feeding on krill, the humpback became the staple catch of New Zealand's shore whaling stations during the twentieth century.

Whaling methods

Ocean whaling in the seas off North Cape, New Zealand, a detail from an etching in J. S. Polack's New Zealand *(1838).*

Three hundred years ago, in the northern hemisphere, the right whale was the species most often hunted by whalers. These whales often swam close to the coast, and could be killed from small boats rowed or sailed out from the shore. In the early eighteenth century however, a group of Nantucket whalers blown offshore encountered and killed a sperm whale. Rendering down the oil of sperm whales produced higher-quality oil than right whales. Sperm whales also had valuable spermaceti oil in their heads. Whaling crews then took to the high seas in large ships to hunt down, kill, and process sperm whales at sea.

Both these types of whaling were carried out in the nineteenth century in New Zealand waters. Shore whaling stations were established up the east coast of the South Island, in Marlborough, on Cook Strait and the Kapiti coast, and in Hawkes Bay and the East Cape. Female right whales were hunted as they moved up the coast in autumn to give birth in areas such as Cloudy Bay and the South Taranaki Bight.

Oceanic or pelagic whalers hunted the sperm whale from large sailing ships. The whalers sometimes took to sea for many months or even years, scouring hunting grounds off the east coast of the South Island and to the north of the North Island. Many of the ocean whalers were Americans from the ports of New England, but there were also 'colonial' (Australian-based), English and French whaleships working the New Zealand 'fishery'.

Some ship owners also performed a cross between shore whaling and ocean whaling, known as bay whaling. Ocean-going whaleships would be based in a bay or harbour and send out boats to catch right whales, as if the operation was based on shore. The ships could then go to sea for the sperm whale season.

Later, shore whaling stations were also established in Northland to target humpback whales.

THE *AUSTRALIAN*

Captain W. B. Rhodes used the barque Australian *for bay whaling, chasing right whales off the east coast of the South Island between June and September 1836. The* Australian *then headed out into the Pacific in search of sperm whales for 18 months — after Rhodes rid himself of several mutinous crew members.*

ALEXANDER TURNBULL LIBRARY

Right whaling — an American ship operates off the coast of New Zealand. Steel engraving from Nimrod of the Sea, *by W. M. Davis (1879).*

Whale Products

In the days when mineral oil and fossil fuels were virtually unknown, whale oil was in high demand for lighting and heating. It was also used in the manufacture of soap, for lubrication and as an agent for tanning leather and waterproofing. Oil rendered from sperm whales was more valuable than that from right whales; the liquid wax or spermaceti from the sperm whale's head was even more highly prized. Spermaceti was a superior lubricant, and also made the best candles, which burnt with a smokeless flame.

The baleen plates from the mouths of right whales are made of strong but flexible protein. This 'whalebone' was used for stiffening corsets and reinforcing seats. The hairs fringing the baleen plates were used for stuffing furniture, and even for making wigs.

A rare but useful whaling by-product was ambergris, a dark-coloured and foul-smelling substance sometimes found deep in the intestines of the sperm whale. When removed from the carcase, or passed by the whale and washed up on beaches, it crystallises, becoming sweet-smelling and the colour of fossilised resin. Ambergris was in great demand for use in perfume manufacture.

The meat of the whale was usually wasted, left on the bones for the sharks. Few whalemen liked the taste of the flesh.

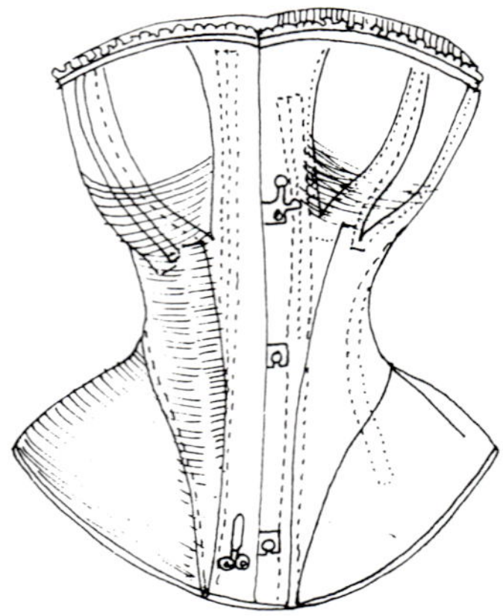

The flexible baleen from the mouths of some whales was highly valued in the making of women's underwear. To achieve the 'wasp' waists of Victorian fashion, women wore corsets braced with strips of baleen to shape their figures. Further strips were used to shape the 'bustles' which padded their skirts behind, and for the series of hoops which made their crinoline dresses stand out like bells.

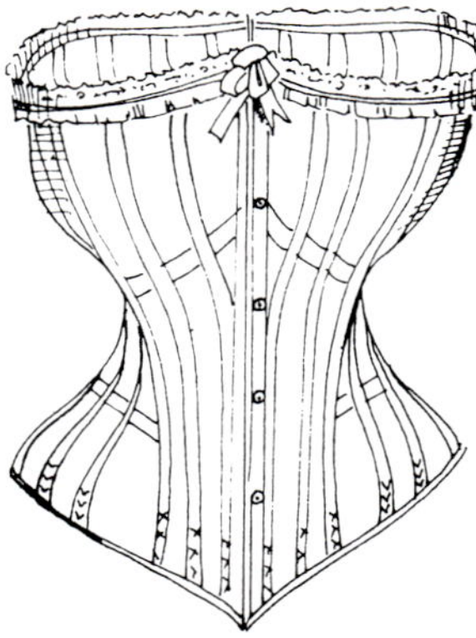

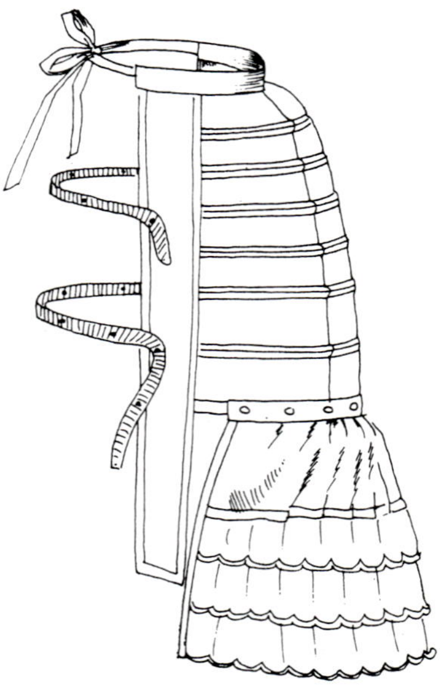

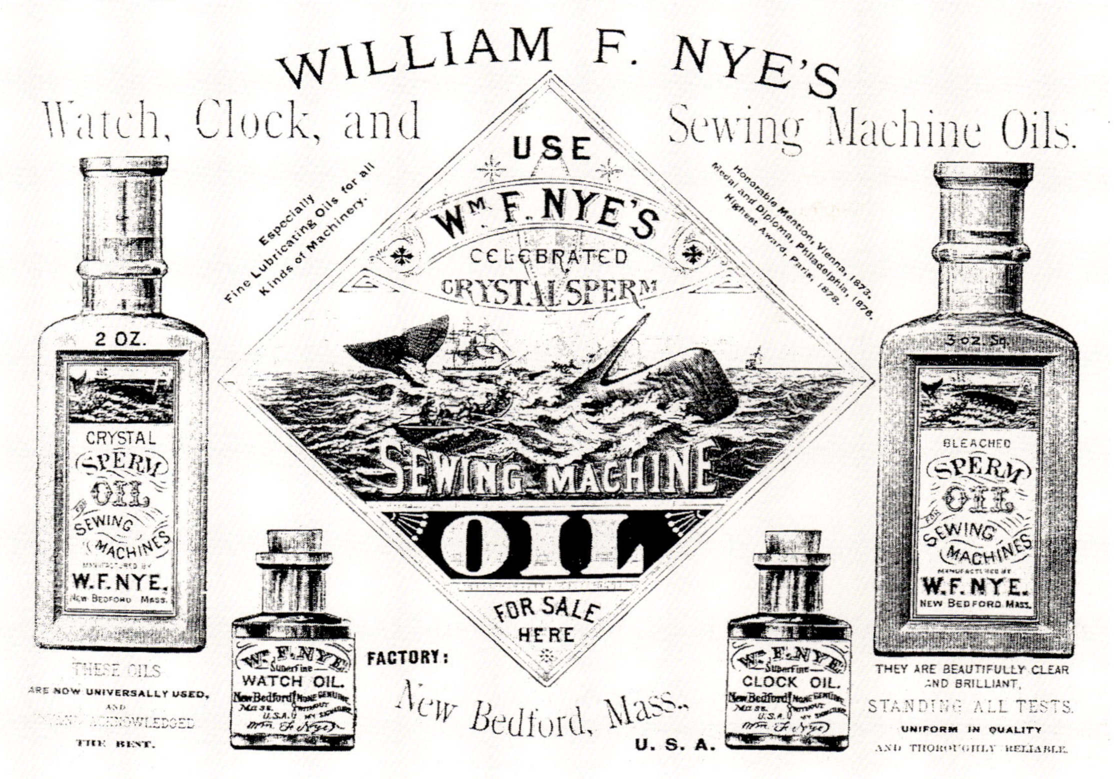

Nineteenth-century advertisement promoting the value of sperm whale oil for lubrication. Fine whale oil was also favoured for use in lamps for it burnt brighter and cleaner than other oils.

SCRIMSHAW

Frantic activity aboard a whaleship was punctuated by hours of idleness, waiting for a whale. To pass the time, the men carved scenes and portraits on sperm whale teeth, called scrimshaw, or made carved boxes and ornaments out of whale bone.

Ocean whaling

The whaling fleets of the world turned their attention to New Zealand little more than 20 years after Cook's visits. Philip Gidley King, the governor of the fast-growing convict colony of New South Wales, was keen to exploit the natural riches of New Zealand. In 1791 he despatched Eber Bunker, a captain from the New England port of Nantucket, to the north of New Zealand in the whaleship *William and Ann*. Bunker found neither flax, the main purpose of the expedition, nor whales, but by the turn of the century a number of British ships were at work on the New Zealand grounds, with varying degrees of success.

In 1802 there were three British whaleships working off the New Zealand coast. In 1809, despite conflicts between Europeans and Maori, there were 12. These ships usually visited the Bay of Islands, using it as a base for reprovisioning, rest and recreation.

The number of visits declined in the 1810s because of war between Britain and the United States, but by the 1820s the British whaleships were back. They were joined by a growing number of colonial (Australian-based) whaling ships, which doubled as general traders in such items as flax and potatoes.

In 1831 a ban excluding American whaleships from Australian ports was lifted, and the New Zealand grounds were soon being worked by ships from the ports of New England, on the north-east coast of the United States. Ships from other countries, including France, Canada, Portugal and Germany, joined them, but the 1830s belonged to the fast, efficient American whaleships and their men. In the peak year of 1839, three-quarters of the 200 or so whaleships working in New Zealand waters were American.

One of the most attractive aspects of whaling here was that New Zealand ports were free of duties and restrictions in the years before British annexation. Visits by foreign whaleships dropped away rapidly after the introduction of British rule in 1840.

BATTLE CRY
'A dead whale or a stove boat' was the battle cry of the whaler, indicating a 'do or die' attitude to the dangerous industry.

SHORE WHALING BASE
Jillett's whaling station on Kapiti Island in 1844, painted by W. A. Bowring around 1907, after an original by J. A. Gilfillan. There were several whaling bases, here, and on adjacent islets and the mainland coast. (See Shore Whaling, from page 33).
ALEXANDER TURNBULL LIBRARY

'THE BAY'
The Bay of Islands was the favourite calling place for whaleships working the oceans about the north of New Zealand. While some ships also used Whangaroa and Mangonui harbours, the Bay of Islands was preferred because of its range of anchorages. In the 1830s the most popular was Kororareka Bay, in front of what is now the township of Russell. Much to the disgust of the missionaries, across the bay at Paihia, entrepreneurs and Maori in Kororareka supplied the whalemen with fresh food, alcohol and female company. Riotous living 'on the beach' soon earned Kororareka the title 'Hellhole of the Pacific'.
'Here Satan maintains his dominion without molestation,' wrote the missionary Rev. Samuel Marsden.
ALEXANDER TURNBULL LIBRARY

1	CAPTAIN'S SHARE	16/240
2	THREE OFFICERS DIVIDE	14/240
3	SIX BOAT-STEERERS DIVIDE	18/240
4	TWENTY CREW DIVIDE	40/240
5	OWNERS AND OVERHEAD	152/240

SHARING THE WHALE

Ocean-going whale crews were taken on for the duration of a voyage, which could be many months or sometimes years. The men were paid in 'lays' or shares of the catch. The size of each man's share was decided before the voyage, according to rank. For example, the master might receive around 1/10 of the total value, the chief mate 1/25, and the ordinary seamen 1/100. The diagram above shows by far the greatest part going to the owners of the whaleship to cover their business costs.

If a whaleship returned to port without catching a single whale — and this did happen — the crewmen would not be paid. They would probably also be in debt to the whaleship owners for advances on items such as clothing and tobacco.

Shore whalers were also paid a lay, but often in alcohol, clothing and tobacco rather than in cash. Some shore whalers also had the value of gear lost or damaged during the season subtracted from their earnings.

ALEXANDER TURNBULL LIBRARY

The Maori and European Whaling

Although there is no evidence that Maori hunted whales before the coming of Europeans, they were quick to join the trade once whaleships began to call at New Zealand ports. From the beginning of the nineteenth century whaleship captains began shipping Maori keen to travel overseas and learn about European tools and technology. Maori were appreciated as skilled seamen and whaling hands, and some rose to positions of responsibility.

The Bay of Islands chief Ruatara, known to whalers and others as 'Duaterra', spent at least four years abroad, from 1805. His voyages took him as far away as Britain. While well-treated by some whalers he was abused by others.

Some Maori were left stranded by unscrupulous whaling captains in Sydney at the end of their voyages, until the governor of New South Wales officially banned the practice in 1805.

Maori tribes in the Bay of Islands and other harbours traded with the whalers: fresh food and firewood in exchange for European goods.

Maori also worked as whalemen at shore stations. Many shore whaling bases were established with the help of a neighbouring Maori tribe. In exchange for trade goods, the Maori would help the whalers build their houses, and protect them from raids by other tribes. Marriages between Maori women and the whalers strengthened these ties.

The first European 'towns' were set up by enterprising traders servicing the visiting whaling ships. Joel Polack, ran this successful trading post in the Bay of Islands in the 1830s.
HOCKEN LIBRARY

Trading with Whalers

RUATARA
While serving with whale ships, Ruatara went to Britain hoping to meet King George the Third, but was unsuccessful. The Rev. Samuel Marsden of the Church Missionary Society befriended Ruatara on his way back from England and took the Maori chief to the mission at Paramatta, near Sydney. For eight months Ruatara studied agriculture there, introducing wheat and other crops to his people when he returned to New Zealand. He also sponsored the establishment of the first Christian mission among his people at Rangihoua in 1814.

The whalers played an important part in the development of early New Zealand. They actively traded with Maori, exchanging blankets, nails and, more significantly, guns for potatoes, pork, firewood and spars.

The northern tribes, in particular, soon gained access to muskets this way. Thus armed, they turned on traditional enemies, making ferocious raids on neighbouring tribes and then tribes further south, as far as Waikato, Hauraki and the Bay of Plenty. During the 1820s, tribal warfare reshaped the Maori politics of the north.

The missionary Reverend Samuel Marsden was encouraged to set up the first mission stations in New Zealand after meeting Maori brought to Sydney by whalemen. Missionaries later mediated between warring tribes to make peace.

'A sperm whale takes the boat'; danger depicted in the Cruise of the Cachalot *by Frank Bullen (1899).*

OCEAN WHALING
Above: 'Boats approaching a whale nearly exhausted'. The sea would seldom be as calm as this. Above right: The harpooner poised to fasten a line to the whale. These hand-coloured etchings are from Foreign Field Sports, Fisheries, Sporting Anecdotes, *1814.*
ALEXANDER TURNBULL LIBRARY

SHORE WHALING
Bottom right: Cutting the blubber off a whale on Mohaka Beach, Hawkes Bay, around 1860. Watercolour by Alfred John Cooper.
ALEXANDER TURNBULL LIBRARY

Whale ships and whaleboats

The whaleships which visited New Zealand were built for strength and endurance, to travel long distances over long periods at sea. They looked functional rather than beautiful, with blunt bows and square sterns. One whaleman observed that they looked as if they had been 'built by the mile and cut off in lengths', and some American whalers unflatteringly called them 'plum pud'ners'. The whaleships were usually three-masted, and varied in size between 200-500 tonnes. The biggest were American and French; the Australian-based ships, which had shorter distances to sail 'home', not so large.

Smaller boats were used in the actual pursuit of the whales, where speed was a critical factor. These whaleboats carried a demountable mast and small sail, although they were also rowed. The whaleboats, which were hung on davits on the ship's side when not in use, were of a fairly universal design, clinker-built and about

Right: Boats from rival ships race for a whale, a sketch from Life and Adventures in the South Pacific, *by A Roving Printer (1861).*
ALEXANDER TURNBULL LIBRARY

Left: The Chance, *a typical New Bedford whaler, with blunt bow and square stern. The first mate, Frank Bullen, based his famous book about ocean whaling on its 'voyage around the world after sperm whales'. This is the frontispiece from his book,* The Cruise of the Cachalot, *first published in 1899.*

EQUIPMENT

The whalers used harpoons not to kill the whale, just to 'fasten' a line to it. Lances were used to kill the whale once it had tired and the boat could approach it. The heads of these lances were leaf-shaped, designed so they could easily be removed from the wound. Also carried aboard the whaleboat was a sharp-edged blubber spade, used on board the main ship to pare off the fat layer but on the smaller boats to sever the tendon of the whale's tail, to stop it from threshing about and smashing the boat. Drogues, made of two heavy pieces of wood attached at right angles, were attached to the line and used as 'sea anchors' to slow the whales down. The boats also carried a regular anchor.

7.5-9m long and 1.5m wide. Despite their shallow draught they were considered extremely seaworthy, but they did not sail well to windward.

Whaleboats were usually manned by six men: the steersman or head man who was in charge and steered the boat with a long oar at the rear; four general oarsmen; and the harpooner at the front, who rowed with the others until the boat closed for the kill.

The boats carried two harpoons, known simply as 'irons' to the whalers. The iron-headed weapons, with a metal shaft a metre or more long attached to a wooden pole, sat in a rack near the bow. The first or main harpoon was fastened to a hemp line of up to 300m in length, carefully coiled into one or two tubs. Once the whale was struck the line had to be able to feed out without kinks or tangles, and without catching up any of the crew.

A second harpoon was attached to the main line as a back-up. If there was not time to fix it to the fleeing whale it was thrown overboard with the line so as not to endanger the crew.

Top: lance.
Bottom: double-barb harpoon.
DRAWINGS: JO KENSINGTON

'There She Blows!'

A look-out kept watch for whales from up the ship's mast. A spout of condensed breath was often the best indicator, as little of a whale's body is usually above the surface of the water. The look-outs also spotted 'white water' made by whales breaching or frolicking. Some whalers claimed they could smell the whales on a calm day.

Once a whale was spotted the cry of 'there she blows', or sometimes just 'there blows' or 'there spouts', would go up, and the whaleboats were launched from the mother ship. Often the whale was sighted several miles from the ship, and would swim even further away with the whalers in pursuit.

Once the whaleboat had rowed or sailed to within range of the whale, as quietly as possible so as not to startle the beast, the harpooner would stow his oar and throw the first iron, attempting to fasten to the whale close behind the left flipper. If there was time, he would then quickly throw the second harpoon too, as insurance.

Once the whale was struck with the harpoons it usually took off at speed, the line running out behind it. Men in the whaleboats had to be very careful not to get caught up in the fast-running rope. If the harpoons held, the crew then shipped their oars and were off on the 'Nantucket sleigh ride', as the boat was pulled along the surface of the water by the injured and enraged whale. Whales

SHIP NAMES

Harry Morton in The Whale's Wake *says each country had its own tradition of naming whaling vessels. British and colonial ships honoured royalty and the aristocracy in names such as* Prince of Wales *and* Earl Spencer. *Americans honoured their presidents with names such as* George Washington *and* Jefferson. *Other ships were named after the whalemen themselves, such as the* Levi Starbuck *and* Bartholomew Gosnold. *And of course many ships were named after wives and families left on shore:* Sarah, Mary, Harriet, Louisa *and many named* Elizabeth.

This ink and watercolour drawing by an unknown artist shows the positions of the whaleboat crew and some of its equipment.
ALEXANDER TURNBULL LIBRARY

could be lost at this stage if the harpoon pulled out, the line broke, or if they dived deeper than the length of line. The end of the line was not tied to the boat, so that extra lengths could be added if required.

Once the whale began to tire, the steersman (usually an officer) and the harpooner swapped places in the whaleboat, so the senior man could strike the mortal blow with the lance. The whaleboat was brought close to the whale, and the lance either thrust at close quarters or thrown, aimed for a vital part such as the heart or lungs. This stage of the operation was perhaps the most dangerous, and many boats were damaged and crews injured, killed outright or drowned, during the whale's death throes. With right whales the greatest danger was the heavy flukes of the tail; with the sperm whales its giant head and fearsome jaws.

The 'Nantucket sleigh ride' — a harpooned whale tows the whaleboat at speed, from The Cruise of the Cachalot *(1899). The ride would have reminded the New Bedford whalers of sledding in the snow.*

TOWING IN

If boats and crew survived the kill unscathed, the whale carcase had then to be towed back to the ship. Sometimes the pull was delayed because of bad weather or darkness, and the whale had to be anchored. Captain W. B. Rhodes wrote in his log of August 1836: 'At 11.30am took the whale in tow with three other boats... At 4.30 anchored the whale, being 20 miles from the ship. The Chief Mate and myself determined to remain all night by the whale. During the night the wind was fresh with a heavy sea, and our situation was not very comfortable at anchor in a whale boat during a cold night twenty miles from land.' Captain Rhodes and the mate eventually made it back to the ship — without the whale — at 7pm the next day, 'pretty well fagg'd after being two days and a night exposed in a whale boat.'

'Cutting In' and 'Trying Out'

Once the carcase was safely back at the ship, the whalers set to work 'cutting in' or flensing — stripping off the layer of blubber. The dead whale was chained to the side of the ship and running tackles set up amongst the rigging. Then two men would be lowered on stages down to the carcase and, with blubber spades, cut a hole in the whale's flesh above one of the side fins. A blubber hook was set into the hole and, using the tackle, the rest of the crew would pull off a long strip of fatty flesh, with much effort. As quickly as the men could cut the edges, strips of blubber were pulled off the carcase, like peeling an orange. Each strip was hoisted high above the ship's deck and lowered into the blubber room below, where the process of trying out the oil began.

The whale's head would be partially severed from the body before cutting in began, so the action of rolling the whale over, as it was 'peeled', twisted off the head. The heads of smaller whales were hoisted on deck, the larger ones lifted higher in the water at the side of the ship. The tongue would be removed for oil extraction. The baleen was cut out of the mouths of right whales. The high-

'STINKERS'

Some whales sank on the journey back to the ship, but their rotting carcases could sometimes be retrieved later when the gases of putrefaction made them rise back to the surface. These 'stinkers' had lost condition and produced less oil, but some oil was better than none. Sometimes the gases of decomposition building up inside the dead whale would cause it to 'burst' or 'explode', before retrieval, or even alongside the ship.

CUTTING IN AND TRYING OUT

Left: The presence of blood and fresh whale flesh in the water often attracted schools of sharks alongside the whaleships while cutting in was in progress. The flensers would sometimes kill a shark with a blow from a blubber spade so the other sharks would feed on their own kind rather than the whale. From Life and Adventures in the South Pacific *by A Roving Printer (1861).*

The engraving at right shows the tryworks in action, in Nimrod of the Sea, *by W. M. Davis (1879).*

ALEXANDER TURNBULL LIBRARY

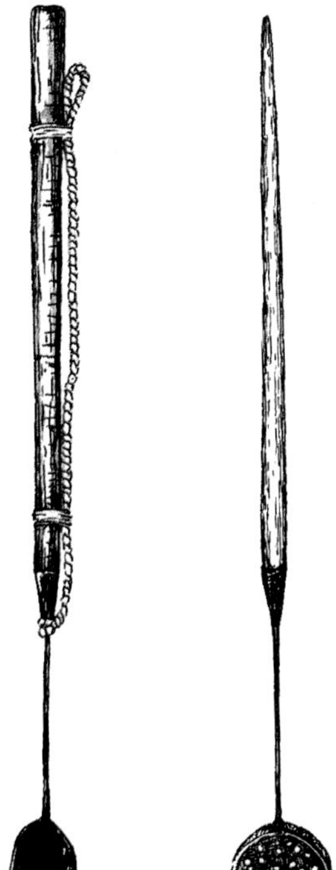

Above: tools of the trade. The blubber spade (left) was used to cut chunks of whale fat from the carcase, while the skimmer (right) was used to remove impurities from the oil.

DRAWINGS: JO KENSINGTON

quality spermaceti oil would be bailed directly out of the cavity in the sperm whale's head. Mostly this was done with a bucket on the end of a pole, but sometimes a man would strip naked and climb inside the whale's head to bail out the oil.

The strips of blubber were cut into chunks in the blubber room. These chunks were then sliced almost all the way through into 'books' or 'Bible leaves'. The smaller the pieces of blubber, the quicker the extraction and the better the quality of oil.

The oil was boiled out of the whale flesh at the tryworks. A large brick furnace, around 2.5m by 3m on the ground and 1.5m high, was built on the deck of the wooden ships between the main and foremasts. Around the tryworks was a channel which the crew kept filled with water to prevent the decks catching on fire. The fires of the tryworks were lit with charcoal and wood, but fed with scraps of blubber from which the oil had been rendered.

Set into the furnace were two or three great cast iron trypots, in which the oil was boiled out of the blubber. The oil was bailed out and put into copper cooling tanks, then decanted into casks.

The process of cutting in the whale and trying out the oil could take several days, depending on the size of the whale. After the whale carcase was stripped of everything of value, it was cast adrift. The crew then set to work cleaning up the ship — unless there was another whale to process.

THE COOPER
The cooper or barrel maker was an important man aboard a whale ship, for it was his task to assemble and maintain the casks in which the whale oil was stored. It was important to prevent any leakage, because oil was money.

PROCESSING AT SEA
The process of cutting in often left the decks greasy with blubber scraps and oil. Trying out the oil created a large amount of black smoke, the soot from which coated the ship's rigging and sails. Fire at sea was also a constant threat. From Life and Adventures in the South Pacific *by A Roving Printer (1861).*
ALEXANDER TURNBULL LIBRARY

The whaling village of Tarwhite, in the outer Marlborough Sounds, sketched by John Wallis Barnicoat in 1843. Tarwhite is a corruption of the Maori name Te Awaiti. The bay was the base, successively, of shore whalers Jacky Guard (1827) and Dicky Barrett (from around 1832).
ALEXANDER TURNBULL LIBRARY

Shore Whaling

As the popularity of ocean whaling in New Zealand waters increased in the 1820s, the first shore whaling stations in New Zealand were becoming established. The seal skin trade had all but died out, and the lowering of British import taxes on 'foreign-caught' whale oil meant Sydney merchants and speculators were keen to hunt the right whale from shore stations in New Zealand. Among the first stations, set up in the late 1820s, were Jacky Guard's Te Awaiti (Tarwhite) on the Tory Channel in the Marlborough Sounds, Preservation Inlet deep in Fiordland, established by Peter Williams, and Port Underwood in Cloudy Bay.

During the 1830s a proliferation of shore stations were established along the Kapiti coast north of Wellington, in the Marlborough Sounds, at Banks Peninsula, in Otago and Southland coast, and on the east coast of the North Island. Some stations lasted only a season and others operated for several years. The most successful stations flourished and enjoyed up to 20 years of success. Most shore stations operated around four boats, employing at least 30 men. Some bases employed up to 70 or 80 men, operating up to 10 boats.

The shore whalers used similar techniques to the ocean whalers in hunting and killing their quarry. Once a whale or whales was spotted from a shore look-out, the whaleboats would be launched from the beach and the chase was on. Skill and speed were required, especially if parties from competing whaling stations were pursuing the same whale. However, the whales were not always killed handy to the station; while a whaling ship could often be moved closer to the kill, the shore whalers were sometimes faced with the arduous task of towing a carcase many miles back to shore. One whale chased from an Otago station was killed so far up the coast the whalers had a hard 26-hour pull to get it home.

Back at the beach the carcase was winched up a slipway and the blubber cut off in chunks by the 'tonguer', a skilled worker who was paid with the oil from the whale's tongue, heart and intestines. The oil was extracted from the blubber in much the same way as it was at sea, by boiling in iron trypots. The carcase, stripped of everything of value, would be towed back out to sea and dumped.

Shore stations were attractive to whalers because they cost less to set up than an ocean whaling operation. While the shore whalers used the same equipment as their deep-sea counterparts to chase, kill and process the whales, there was not the major outlay of buying a 'mother ship'.

Whalers pose at Te Awaiti in the Marlborough Sounds in the 1890s. The farther whaleboat is the Swiftsure, *now in the Canterbury Museum.*
S. WILLIAMS COLLECTION, ALEXANDER TURNBULL LIBRARY

Most shore stations were run in connection with a trading ship, which would bring in supplies and take the oil and baleen to the Sydney market at the end of the season. The oil was often of better quality than that obtained at sea because it had spent less time in the cask, and the barrels were less likely to leak. General maintenance was less of a problem ashore than at sea. While at a shore station buildings may have burnt down, and in one case been washed away by an unusually high tide, there was little or no risk of a total loss such as the sinking or burning of a whaling ship.

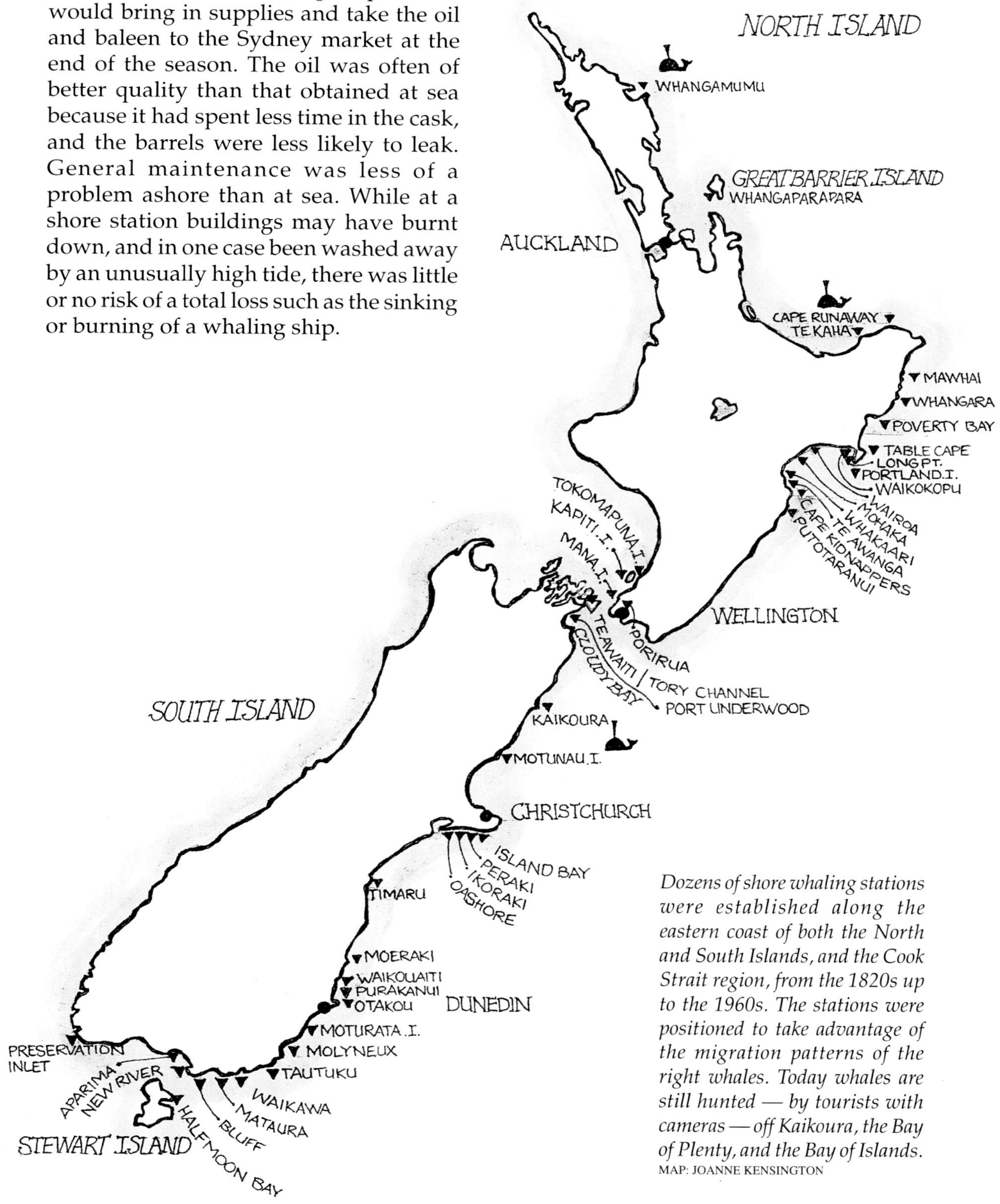

Dozens of shore whaling stations were established along the eastern coast of both the North and South Islands, and the Cook Strait region, from the 1820s up to the 1960s. The stations were positioned to take advantage of the migration patterns of the right whales. Today whales are still hunted — by tourists with cameras — off Kaikoura, the Bay of Plenty, and the Bay of Islands.
MAP: JOANNE KENSINGTON

The shore whalers

The shore whalers were among the first permanent European settlers in New Zealand. As well as being based around the coast during the winter whaling season, many also stayed at the small settlements during the summer.

Life for the shore whalers was rough, but a good deal more comfortable than ocean whaling. Whalers who lived full-time in New Zealand often started small farms during the summer season, raising pigs and crops for food and trade. Many became allied with or married into a local tribe, ensuring protection for the Europeans and trade for the Maori. Many whalers lived with Maori women and began families. Some of these marriages were later made legal by visiting missionaries.

A whaler's 'wife' was expected to cook, wash and mend his clothes, and keep the house in order. In exchange the whaler would clothe her, give a portion of his income to her family, and support her tribe. 'These whalers' wives are generally distinguished by a strong affection for their companion; are very quick in acquiring habits of order and cleanliness; facilitate the intercourse between the whalers and their own countrymen; and often manage to obtain a strong influence over the wild passions of the former,' Edward Jerningham Wakefield wrote.

Although many shore stations were set up on beautiful beaches and bays, the nature of the industry often made them unattractive to outsiders. The camps often smelled strongly of whale oil, flesh and spent blubber — exceeded only, according to one observer, by the smell of rum.

Some missionaries viewed the shore stations as places of wickedness and immorality. Wesleyan missionary John Bumby accused the whalers at one station of practising 'every species of iniquity without restraint and without concealment.... The very soil is polluted.' Many contemporary observers record that the whalers drank a lot of alcohol, and behaved somewhat riotously when drunk, but when engaged in the business of whaling they were hard-working and disciplined.

'The frankness and manly courage of the sailor mingle with the cunning and reckless daring of the convict or "lag", in no common manner,' Wakefield noted. 'Though prone to drunkenness and its attendant evils, the whaler is hospitable in the extreme, and his rough-built house is a model of cleanliness and order.... His want of book-

WHALER'S NAMES

The shore whalemen often obtained colourful nicknames, such as Butcher Nott, Flash Bill, Long Bob, Gipsy Smith and Fat Jackson. Joseph Thoms, who ran stations at Te Awaiti and Paremata, was more commonly known as Geordie Bolts, which may have been his real name. The whalers also had their own slang, calling pigs grunters, guns shooting sticks, and blankets spreaders.

EDWARD JERNINGHAM WAKEFIELD (1820-1879)

The son of the founder of the New Zealand Company wrote a lively record of his time as a Company agent in 1839-40. At the age of 19, Wakefield travelled widely in New Zealand, looking for places to settle British emigrants. His book Adventures in New Zealand *(1845) includes frank descriptions of Maori and European life prior to the signing of the Treaty of Waitangi.*

Whaler's house at Kaikoura, an etching by William Francis Barraud in Made In New Zealand.
ALEXANDER TURNBULL LIBRARY

learning is counteracted by a considerable knowledge of the world.'

The shore whalers' houses were generally built with help from the Maori, thatched with reeds and rushes or made of wattle and daub over a wooden frame. 'A huge chimney nearly fills one end of the house; and [the house] generally swarms with natives, iron pots and kettles, favourite dogs, and joints of the whale's backbone, which serve as stools,' Wakefield wrote. '...Bunks with neat curtains line the greater part of the sides of the house. A large deal table and two long benches stand in the middle of the hard earthern floor.... Two or three of the Maori are asleep, rolled in their blankets against the sunny wall; and a few half-caste children are playing with the goats or hallooing at the fowls and pigeons on the oily beach before the house.'

Port Underwood on Cloudy Bay, Marlborough, was a popular base for shore whalers. John Guard's second shore whaling station was established at Kakapo Bay, within the long harbour. Guard's house is in the centre of this picture painted by William Fox.
HOCKEN LIBRARY

Jacky Guard (?1792-1857)

John or Jacky Guard is generally credited with the establishment of shore whaling in New Zealand, although the date is sometimes disputed. Guard was transported to New South Wales in 1815 for stealing a quilt, and took up sealing when he finished his time in 1820. While on a sealing expedition in 1827, Guard was driven to shelter from a gale in what is now known as Tory Channel, in the Marlborough Sounds. The crew settled at Te Awaiti and carried on sealing and whaling. Without the necessary equipment they were unable to save the oil, so killed whales for their baleen only. Life was rough — the neighbouring Maori frequently burnt down their huts, and sometimes the crew resorted to eating whale meat and wild turnip tops.

Guard returned to Sydney to marry young Elizabeth (Betty) Parker, and brought her to Te Awaiti. Just 16 years old, she gave birth to their son John Guard Junior at Te Awaiti on October 1, 1831. He was the first European child born in the South Island.

Around 1832 Guard moved base to Kakapo Bay, Port Underwood, which opens onto Cloudy Bay. The Guards visited Sydney in 1834 but on the way home the ship was driven ashore in Taranaki. The castaways were attacked by local Maori and Betty, John Jnr and daughter Louisa were held to ransom. They were rescued after four months by soldiers despatched from Sydney; an enquiry was later held into the use of excessive force during the rescue.

Despite this and other clashes with local Maori, the Guards prospered at Kakapo Bay and their descendants still live there today.

Dicky Barrett (?1797-1847)

Dicky Barrett's first hotel was a centre of community life in early Wellington. His name remained attached to a hotel there into the 1980s. Barrett's Reef at the entrance to Port Nicholson remains a hazard to shipping, as it was when Barrett piloted the first New Zealand Company ships into the harbour more than 150 years ago. Detail from a hand-coloured engraving by Henry Melville after S. C. Brees in Pictorial Illustrations of New Zealand *(1847).*
ALEXANDER TURNBULL LIBRARY

The best-known of the shore whalers was Richard 'Dicky' Barrett, known to the Maori as Tiki Parete. He first came to New Zealand as a trader in 1827 with partner Jacky Love, and settled on the Taranaki coast. He married a high-ranking Maori woman, which gave him good connections with the Te Ati Awa (Ngati Awa) tribe.

Barrett and Love took over operations at Jacky Guard's Te Awaiti shore whaling station on Tory Channel around 1832. When the advance party of New Zealand Company officials arrived to settle at Port Nicholson, Barrett was engaged as an interpreter and pilot, bringing the ship *Tory* safely past the reef at the entrance to Wellington Harbour which still bears his name. He also aided in the purchase of land at Port Nicholson, Queen Charlotte Sound and Taranaki.

Barrett opened Wellington's first hotel in 1840. It was one of the most important buildings in the colony, a social and business meeting-place, until it was destroyed in an earthquake in 1855.

Barrett moved back to Taranaki in 1841 and operated another whaling station on Moturoa Island, the innermost of the Sugar Loaves, off what is now New Plymouth. Although by all accounts he was rather too fat to be actively whaling, he was injured at sea in 1846 when the tail of a harpooned whale struck his boat. Although not badly injured, he never completely recovered and died the next year.

Johnny Jones (?1808-1869)

Johnny Jones of Waikouaiti on the North Otago coast was one of the few shore whalers to make a fortune from the trade. Jones was a 'currency lad', born in Sydney, who owned shares in three whaling vessels by his 21st birthday. In 1835 he went into partnership with Edwin Palmer to buy a whaling station at Preservation Inlet, Fiordland and a cargo ship, the *Sydney Packet*.

The station — and Jones — flourished. He bought more land and ships and expanded his whaling empire. In 1838 he purchased his best-known station, Waikouaiti, on the Otago coast, for £225 after its previous owners failed. In 1839 he reported to the New South Wales government that he operated seven whaling stations in New Zealand, employing 280 men.

Jones was not hurt by the downturn in the whaling trade in the 1840s, having also invested in land and founded a small farming settlement at Waikouaiti. He also did well trading with the new settlement of Dunedin from 1848. Jones, his wife Sarah and their children, moved to Dunedin in 1854 and prospered in the shipping trade.

Johnny Jones.
HOCKEN LIBRARY.

Thomas Evans

Captain Tommy Evans, 'The Old Man', ran what was considered the most efficient and successful whaling station on the Kapiti coast, north of Wellington. Evans' station on Tokomapuna Island, inshore of Kapiti Island, was run with military precision. His whalers wore a uniform of red or blue worsted shirts with white binding on the seams, white trousers and sou'westers. Their whaling equipment was covered with green canvas sheets when not in use. Evans' own whaling boat was painted a flesh colour with a red nose, adorned with the emblem of the Prince of Wales feather. Its name, *Saucy Jack*, was painted near the stern.

Evans' regime of order and discipline seems to have paid off: in 1840 his station took more than half the oil collected in the area. But Evans' men were similar to other whalers in some respects: when Wakefield visited at Christmas 1840 he observed that all but a few of the men were drunk.

Edward Jerningham Wakefield, who visited Evans' station in 1840, observed that the men were expected to work hard. 'I have seen boats from Kapiti at Horowhenua, a distance of fifteen miles to windward, half an hour after daylight. And the whole distance is rowed without a rest; it is not until arrived on the ground selected for the day that the headsman allows them to peak their oars and light a pipe.'

The Decline of Whaling

By the 1840s right whales were becoming increasingly scarce in New Zealand waters. One by one the shore stations faltered and closed, with most ceasing to operate by the 1850s.

Ocean whaling continued in New Zealand waters, at a reduced level, for several more decades. The number of foreign ships visiting New Zealand ports dropped with British annexation and the introduction of customs duties in 1840. Gold rushes, starting in California in 1849, drew young men away from the whaling trade, and the development of the American west drew attention away from the New England whaling ports. The American Civil War from 1861-65 sounded the final toll.

By this time the colonisation of New Zealand was well underway, with towns springing up and land being cleared for farming. The wild old days of whaling and sealing on the New Zealand coast were over.

The ruins of Johnny Jones's whaling station on the beach at Waikouaiti. Note the remains of a trypot for boiling down blubber (left) and a windlass for winding in a hauling rope (right). The farm buildings of Matanaka on the cliffs above have been maintained, however, as an historic place (see page 45).
HOCKEN LIBRARY

Twentieth-century Whaling

Modern whaling, from motor-powered boats and using harpoon guns, began in New Zealand in 1910. Up until this time whaling had been in a slump, but three or four commercial enterprises now sprang up. Rorquals such as humpback whales had not previously been targetted by whalers because they were fast-swimming and sank when dead.The new technology made it possible to successfully pursue these species.

The Cook family's station, established in 1890 at Whangamumu Harbour, just outside the Bay of Islands, was the first to use a steam-powered whale chaser, in

WHALING AT TE KAHA
Maori farmers in the eastern Bay of Plenty supplemented their income by occasional shore whaling, into the 1930s. They used traditional nineteenth century methods, rowing their whaleboats and harpooning by hand.

'Modern launches from the Tory Channel whaling station race after a whale'.
PHOTOGRAPH: *WEEKLY NEWS*
MAKING NEW ZEALAND COLLECTION, ALEXANDER TURNBULL LIBRARY

1910. Parties from this station also spent seasons at a whaling base on Campbell Island.

The Whangamumu station had an unusual way of catching humpback whales, before killing them with harpoon guns. A steel wire net was set across a channel through which the whales passed, entangling them and slowing them down for the whalers to shoot. The Whangamumu station was closed in 1933.

The year after the Cooks turned to steam power, Joe Perano began his operation on the Tory Channel, at the entrance to the Marlborough Sounds. Here humpback whales were driven into the narrow entrance of the channel by motorised whale chasers, and slaughtered. Several other whaling stations competed with the Peranos in the 1910s, and Joe's brother Charlie operated a rival station from Tipi Bay. The competition between the brothers was fierce until Joe Perano took over Charlie's operation in 1927.

The Perano whaling operating persisted to the very end of commercial whaling in New Zealand. Despite a peak season in 1960 when 226 whales were killed, the humpback whale population was in sharp decline. Whale oil prices were also falling, and the industry finally faltered when the Government refused to subsidise the purchase of sperm whale oil. The last whale killed commercially in New Zealand waters, a bull sperm, was harpooned on December 21, 1964.

Other stations operated at Kaikoura until 1921, and at Whangaparapara on Great Barrier Island until 1962. The station manager at Whangaparapara was Charlie Heberley, the great-great-grandson of whaler James 'Worser' Heberley, after whom Wellington's Worser Bay is named.

'Fighting whales with the most modern equipment demands great skill in the operation of the harpoon gun.' Whalers from the Tory Channel station in action.
PHOTOGRAPH: H. FARMER MCDONALD
MAKING NEW ZEALAND COLLECTION,
ALEXANDER TURNBULL LIBRARY

Trypot used by whalers to 'try' the blubber from a whale. Used on land, they were similar to the trypots carried on the deck of an ocean whaling ship. Strips of blubber were boiled up in the trypot to separate the oil, which was poured off. While this pot was photographed at Paremata, on the Kapiti coast, around 1900, they may still be seen today at old whaling sites and museums.
CROMPTON-SMITH COLLECTION, ALEXANDER TURNBULL LIBRARY

Relics of the Whaling Days

The sealing gangs of the late eighteenth and early nineteenth centuries left few signs of their occupation of New Zealand. The whalers left more relics of their enterprise, however. The towns of Akaroa on Banks Peninsula and Russell in the Bay of Islands began in the whaling days. Fyffe House in Kaikoura was built by a shore whaler, George Fyffe, about 1860. On Stewart Island, Acker's Cottage stands on the beach at Halfmoon Bay. Remains of whaling stations can also be seen at Whangamumu in Northland, on Great Barrier Island and on Kapiti Island. The remains of the Perano station on Tory Channel can be seen from the inter-island ferry.

Hauling a whale up the slip at the Whangamumu whaling station, just outside the Bay of Islands. The station closed in 1933.
ADMIRAL J. ROSS COLLECTION, ALEXANDER TURNBULL LIBRARY

Restored by the Historic Places Trust, Fyffe House in Kaikoura is partly supported by foundations made of whale vertebrae. Originally a faintly pink hue was apparent in its paint, a mixture of whale oil and red and white lead.

PHOTOGRAPHS: GORDON ELL

Farm buildings at Matanaka, once the base of shore whaler Johnny Jones at Waikouaiti, north Otago. The buildings are preserved by the Historic Places Trust.

Although there is no road access, the ruins of the Whangamumu whaling station can be reached by cruising boats and trampers.

Whales today

Because it was such a popular and easy prey for the whalemen, and because mainly female animals and calves were killed, the right whale is now one of the rarest whales in the world. Scientists estimate there are only a few thousand southern right whales left, with around 150 breeding in sub-Antarctic waters south of New Zealand. The species was slow to recover from the slaughter of the 1830s-40s, and it has recently been revealed that whaleships from the former Soviet Union illegally killed more than 3000 right whales in the 1950s and 60s.

Sperm whales are more numerous, with estimates varying from 290,000 to as many as 1.5 million worldwide. Sperm whale populations were not as greatly affected by hunting, because the whalers targeted the larger bulls. Each group of female sperm whales mates with just one bull, leaving many 'bachelors', so many of those killed were not breeding males.

The humpback whale, hunted in New Zealand until the 1960s, is rarer: best estimates around 20,000 worldwide, with an estimated 12,000 in southern waters (about 10% of their estimated population in 1900).

WHALE STRANDINGS

Strandings, especially of smaller species of whales and dolphins, are relatively common on the New Zealand coastline, exciting public interest and sympathy. Whales seem to strand for several reasons: if they are old or sick, having difficulty with calving, or if they make a navigational mistake. Mass strandings of toothed whales such as pilot whales are often triggered by an individual whale in distress, its calls attracting the rest of the pod close to shore. Below, a whale rescue team has covered a beached 'pod' and keeps them damp until they can be returned to sea by the rising tide.
DEPARTMENT OF CONSERVATION.

Strandings and sightings

Today many people are lucky enough to see whales in the waters around New Zealand. Right whales are no longer regularly seen about the New Zealand coast, but a tourist industry has been based on the regular visits of sperm whales and other cetaceans to the deep waters off Kaikoura, on the east coast of the South Island.

Four species of dolphin are still common around our coast, as are larger toothed whales such as orca (killer whales) and pilot whales.

Bryde's (pronounced broo-dahs) whales, a fairly large species of baleen whale growing up to 14m, are quite common off the east coast of the North Island from the Bay of Plenty north. Smaller baleen whales such as minke and sei whales may also be seen at sea.

Blue and humpback whales are occasional but spectacular visitors.

The Department of Conservation is responsible for the protection of New Zealand's marine mammals, and manages whale strandings and rescues. D.o.C should be contacted immediately in the event of a stranding.

All whales and dolphins, as well as seals, are fully protected by the Marine Mammals Protection Act (1978). The Marine Mammals Protection Regulations (1992) set rules for behaviour around the animals.

On December 6, 1994, the Southern Ocean Whale Sanctuary was established by the International Whaling Commission, banning commercial whaling south of a line at 40° South (around the latitude of Wanganui), and dipping around the South American continent. A similar prohibition is in force in the Indian Ocean.

The only nations still taking part in major commercial whaling enterprises are Japan and Norway.

KEEPING WHALES ALIVE

If a stranding occurs in a remote area, it may be some time before Department of Conservation staff arrive to help the whales. These important steps can mean the difference between life and death for stranded whales:

- *check the whale's blowhole is clear and above water, so it can breathe.*
- *keep the whale cool, by pouring water over it. Cover its skin with damp cloths or newspaper to protect it from the sun.*
- *if possible, keep the weight of the whale off its flippers, which can easily be damaged.*

Do not attempt to move the whale, poke or shove it, or make loud noises. Talk to it — whales in distress seem to be comforted by humans.

Right: A whale rescue team keeps a stranded whale afloat and breathing as the tide rises.
DEPARTMENT OF CONSERVATION.

SPERM WHALES
Sperm whales are resident off the Kaikoura coast year-round, feeding on fish and squid in a deep under-sea canyon which comes to within 2km of the shore. Tour guides find the whales by watching for their spouts, and using an underwater listening device called a hydrophone.
COURTESY WHALE WATCH KAIKOURA LTD.

Seeing whales and dolphins

Kaikoura, on the north-east coast of the South Island, was an important shore whaling base from the 1840s right up until the 1920s. People are still chasing whales there today, but now they come not to kill but to watch these magnificent creatures. Because of the underwater geography of the area, Kaikoura is frequently visited by sperm whales, dolphins and other cetaceans. Commercial 'whale watching' trips began from Kaikoura in 1987, and now more than 40,000 tourists, mainly from overseas, visit the small town each year to view the whales.

Other whale watching tours are now based in the Bay of Islands and the Bay of Plenty. Dolphins, and other smaller whales such as Bryde's whales, can be seen quite close to shore in these areas.

NAMING THE WHALES
Individual sperm whales can be identified by particular physical characteristics, such as the shape of their tail flukes. At least 20 sperm whales have been given names by tour guides at Kaikoura, and are seen regularly. The whales here are mainly 'teenage' bachelor males, not attached to a pod of breeding females. Fourteen other species of whales and dolphins have also been spotted off Kaikoura, including Hector's and dusky dolphins, orca (killer whales) and pilot whales.
COURTESY WHALE WATCH KAIKOURA LTD.